GW00982535

Gallery Books
Editor Peter Fallon

CHRIST DELIVER US!

Thomas Kilroy

CHRIST DELIVER US!

after Wedekind's
Spring Awakening

Gallery Books

Christ Deliver Us!
is first published
simultaneously in paperback
and in a clothbound edition
on the day of its première,
16 February 2010.

The Gallery Press
Loughcrew
Oldcastle
County Meath
Ireland

© Thomas Kilroy 2010

ISBN 978 1 85235 488 6 *paperback*
        978 1 85235 489 3 *clothbound*

A CIP catalogue record for this book
is available from the British Library.

Thomas Kilroy has asserted his right to
be identified as the author of this Work.

All rights whatsoever are strictly reserved.
Requests to reproduce the text in whole or in
part should be addressed to the publishers.
Application for performance in any medium
must be made in advance, prior to the
commencement of rehearsals, and for
translation into any language, to
Alan Brodie Representation Ltd,
Fairgate House, 78 New Oxford Street,
London WC1A 1HB.

Setting
A provincial Irish city with its own Diocesan College (Secondary School) and its own Industrial School for 'difficult' boys.

Time
Late 1940s/early 1950s.

Characters

Teenagers
WINNIE BUTLER
MONICA and TESS, *her friends*
MICHAEL GRAINGER
MOSSY LANNIGAN
VIVIE

College Boys
SHELLY
CAREY
LINK
COADY

Industrial School Boys
MAHON ('GOUGER')
O'NEILL ('RATSER')
SHEA ('BLADE')
BULGER

Parents
MRS BUTLER
MR GRAINGER
MRS GRAINGER

Priests
THE CANON
FR SEAMUS
FR JACK
FR JOSEPH
FR KIERAN

Christian Brothers
FIRST CHRISTIAN BROTHER
SECOND CHRISTIAN BROTHER

Christ Deliver Us! was first performed in the Abbey Theatre, Dublin, on Tuesday, 16 February 2010, with the following cast:

WINNIE BUTLER	Aoife Duffin
TESS	Liz Fitzgibbon
MONICA	Caoilfhionn Dunne
VIVIE	Ruth McGill
MICHAEL GRAINGER	Aaron Monaghan
MOSSY LANNIGAN	Laurence Kinlan
MRS BUTLER	Eleanor Methven
MRS GRAINGER	Cathy Belton
FR SEAMUS	Tom Hickey
THE CANON	Denis Conway
FR JOSEPH	Peter Hanly
FR KIERAN/MR GRAINGER	Michael McElhatton
FR JACK/	
SECOND CHRISTIAN BROTHER	Karl Quinn
PREFECT/	
FIRST CHRISTIAN BROTHER	Diarmaid Murtagh

BOYS
Keith Burke, Gavin Fullam, Seamus Brennan, Eamonn Owens, Brian Bennett, Robert Bannon, Sean Flanagan, Simon Boyle, Stephen O'Rourke

Director	Wayne Jordan
Set Design	Naomi Wilkinson
Lighting Design	Sinéad Wallace
Costume Design	Joan O'Clery
Composer	Caoimhín O Raghallaigh
Choreography	Colin Dunne
Sound	Ben Delaney
Fight Director	Paul Burke
Assistant Director	Tara Robinson
Voice Director	Andrea Ainsworth
CSM	Anne Kyle
DSM	Stephen Dempsey
ASM	Orla Burke

for my daughter, Hannah May Kilroy

ACT ONE

The stage is on two levels. The lower level, downstage, is the main acting area, the world of the three young teenagers, WINNIE, MICHAEL *and* MOSSY. *The upper level is used for more public scenes such as the college, the Industrial School, cemetery etc. This area is dominated by a high, grim wall which becomes the tower of the final scenes.*

Lights up on upper level: A Diocesan College. Sound of a piercing bell. A group of schoolboys rush on, gathering beneath the wall. They furtively light up cigarettes. They walk back and forth beneath the wall in twos, dragging on the hidden cigarettes in the palms of their hands. A schoolboy rushes on and hisses, gesticulating off. Cigarettes hastily stubbed out.

A prefect, a clerical student, early 20s, in clerical black, soutane, biretta, coat, briskly on. He observes the walking boys, turns, leaves. They are about to light up again when he comes back on again, very quickly, this time accompanied by FR JOSEPH *carrying a cane. The boys are lined up and a caning on the hands begins by the priest, six wallops to each hand. Lights down as the beatings continue.*

Sounds up of spectators, off, watching a game of hurling, roars and shouts: 'C'mon Joseph's!', 'Get it, Kelly!', 'G'man Murphy, bate the hell outta him!'

A flare of bright light brings a new dynamism on stage: a highly choreographed sequence of boys hurling. Four boys in contrasting black and white/green and white jerseys, togs, socks and boots. First they compete for a throw-in, hurleys clashing for the ball between their feet. One raises the ball, catches it in his hand and tries to strike it. He is hooked by one of the others and the ball is at their feet again, hurleys clashing once more. Then the ball is tossed upwards, over their heads, and they rise together, hurleys clashing aloft over their heads as they leap. One of them connects and all four watch the ball flying away. Then they run off in pursuit of the ball to more shouts of encouragement.

Lower level. Slow lights up on the Butler kitchen. WINNIE, *a pretty fifteen-year-old and her mother, mid-50s.* WINNIE *is holding up a dress for her mother.*

WINNIE (*Dress*) You've gone and made it longer, Mammy. What'd ya do that for?

MRS BUTLER You're still growing, Winnie.

WINNIE It's ruined, so 'tis! Look at the cut of it! Who wants to get bigger if it means ruining something lovely?

MRS BUTLER It's not a bit ruined. You can't go round for the rest of your life in a doll's dress.

WINNIE I'd take a doll's dress any day a' the week instead of a yoke that looks like someone's nightshirt. Please, Mammy! Just let me keep it the way it was. Please! Just till summer. Then I'll be sixteen and you can dress me up like a scarecrow for all I care.

MRS BUTLER Do you know, I used to be the same at your age. Never wanting to grow up. Where did it all go, I ask ya?

WINNIE I want to be grown up. It's just I want everything to stay — beautiful, like. OK?

MRS BUTLER You can twist me round your little finger, Winnie. God knows what you'll be like when you do grow up.

WINNIE Maybe I won't grow up at all. Ever.

MRS BUTLER What'd ya say?

WINNIE 'S nothing.

MRS BUTLER (*Upset*) Is so! I just hate it when you talk that way, Winnie — hate it! Flying in the face of God, saying terrible things like that —

WINNIE Sorry — Sorry.

MRS BUTLER 'Clare to God I don't know where such talk comes from!

WINNIE Said sorry! Alright?

MRS BUTLER Frighten me, so you do —

WINNIE Don't mean to frighten you, Mammy. 'Tis the way it comes outta me mouth, like.

MRS BUTLER (*Kissing her*) Here. We'll say no more about it, so.

WINNIE   It's only when I can't sleep at night I get these
         — y'know? It's like everything has come to an
         end. Nothing left at all. Do you think that's a
         sin, Mammy? To be thinking that way?

         *Her mother looks at her, not·knowing what to
         say. Then she grabs the dress.*

MRS BUTLER   Here! Gimme that! Let me take off that auld
             hem altogether.
WINNIE   Other times I go in the other direction entirely
         — thinking everything's grand and that there's
         nothing bad in the world. Up and down, up and
         down. You must think I'm raving, Mammy?
MRS BUTLER   I think ye're a precious angel, that's what I
             think. Now the others are all gone outta the
             house you're all I have. Ya can wear what ya
             like. Just as long as you don't catch yer death
             a' cold.
WINNIE   But it's nearly summer, Mammy! I just love
         having me legs bare. I love to feel the air on me
         skin. It's like — drinking something scrump-
         tious. That's the opposite of getting sick, in't it?
         I feel so great! You should thank your lucky
         stars, Mammy, that I don't just throw off all me
         clothes! Just like that! And, you know some-
         thing else? I could be wearing rags and I'd still
         feel like a princess underneath. (*She pirouettes*)
         Oh, don't look so shocked, Mammy! Nobody
         can ever know how I really feel underneath.
         Nobody!

         Her mother watches her, worriedly. WINNIE
         twirls slowly, lost. MRS BUTLER *looks at the
         dress in her hands and the lights come down on
         both of them.*
             *Lights up on upper level as before, boys walk-
         ing, two by two, back and forth by the wall.*
         MOSSY *and* MICHAEL, *fifteen- or sixteen-year-*

olds, wheel their bicycles on downstage. Three boys run forward towards MOSSY *and* MICHAEL.

SHELLY   Hey, Mossy! Are ya goin' home? Will ya buy some fags for me downtown?

CAREY   Ye're not supposed to be talking to day-boys, Shelly, after class.

SHELLY   Feck off, Carey! (*To* MOSSY) Will ya, Mossy?

MOSSY   What d'ya want, so?

SHELLY   Packet a' Craven A. (*To third boy*) Hey, Link! Will ya go halves on a packet a' ten?

LINK   Shag off, Shelly, I have me own fags.

SHELLY   (*Throwing coins*) Catch, so!

MOSSY   Hey, there's only a couple of threepenny bits here.

CAREY & LINK   (*Jeering*) Fork it out, Shelly! G'wan awr that, Shelly!

SHELLY   (*Throwing more coins*) Jays! I'm broke!

CAREY   Hey, lads, will ya get us a bar of Cadbury's while ye're at it?

MOSSY   What d'ya think we are? Is it messenger boys? Let's go, Michael —

CAREY & LINK   (*To* MOSSY) Go on with ya, Lannigan! Ye're only a suck, Lannigan! Ye're only an auld shite!

MICHAEL   Lave him alone!

MICHAEL *and* MOSSY *cycle off. Lights down on boys by the wall.*
    Bright light on the other side of the stage and into the light stroll WINNIE *and her pals,* MONICA, *who is moody, and plump* TESS.

MONICA   Don't ye just love this weather?

WINNIE   It's what the sun does to yer skin, the burning — for hours after —

TESS   It's too feckin' hot for me, I can tell ya. Aren't ye roasted, the pair of ye?

WINNIE   Ye're goin' to hafta lose a few pounds, Tess, me love.

TESS   Who're ya tellin'! Ma says I'm getting like a turkey.

WINNIE   Let's go up the river, girls. Ya never know who we might run into. Did ye see the raft the lads put out? They say Michael Grainger nearly drowned off it.

MONICA   That fella thinks he's posh, so he does —

TESS   But isn't he a fierce swimmer, Michael Grainger, like?

WINNIE   Don't matter. That wouldn't stop him being drownded. There's always something in the world that's stronger than us. (*The others look at her, puzzled*) Then you just have to — give in to it! Surrender! I said the same thing to Michael Grainger, so I did!

         The other two look at one another, still confused.
         WINNIE *marches off. They follow.*
         Immediate lights up on MICHAEL *leading* MOSSY *as they cycle downstage. They throw down bicycles and school bags, and sit. The effect from now on is cross-cutting between the boys and girls at either side of the stage.*

MICHAEL You're a right auld softie, Mossy, with them fellas, so y'are. Cadbury's how are ya!

MOSSY   I feel fierce sorry for them boarders, Michael. Locked up in that place day and night. Least we get to go home after school. There was another fierce fight in the Senior Dorm the other night. I'd go outta me mind if I had to put up with that sorta stuff, fightin' 'n stuff.

MICHAEL Ya'll get six of the stick on either hand if ye're caught buying them fags.

MOSSY   Don't care what happens to me anymore, so I don't. (*Pause*) What are ya thinking about, Michael?

MICHAEL Oh, just what ya said. What's the point of it all?

MOSSY   D'ya mean school?

MICHAEL   I mean life. I mean why we're in the world at all. It means — nothing!

MOSSY   Last time ya said something like that it made me feel terrible for weeks.

MICHAEL   Nothing at all —

MOSSY   And now I have them headaches back again. Could I ask ya something, Michael?

MICHAEL   Fire ahead.

MOSSY   D'ya think am I any good?

MICHAEL   Any good at what?

MOSSY   Just any good, full stop. Sometimes I think I'm no good for anything at all. And I feel sort of ashamed all the time, so I do. Why do I feel ashamed like that, Michael?

MICHAEL   It's the way we're born.

MOSSY   It's priests.

MICHAEL   Naw, it's the way we came into the world. Suppose you wanted to strip off, now — you wouldn't be able to. That's not priests. It's something else entirely. Even if you're all alone with your best friend. Unless, of course, he was to strip at the same time.

MOSSY   I hate that feckin' college. Michael, I — I failed the mock maths.

MICHAEL   How d'ya know? That ya failed?

MOSSY   Oh, I know. Michael, I have to tell ya something. I changed the paper.

MICHAEL   Ya what?! Jays!

MOSSY   I stole into the room of the Spirit Lamp and changed the calculus to the right answer. D'ya think he'll notice? The Spirit Lamp?

MICHAEL   Ya mean Father Jimmy? Ya went in his room and changed the sums! I didn't think ya had it in ya.

MOSSY   (*Quickly*) Don't tell! I had to do it! I had to! If I failed, me father'd lather me. He's a killer, so he is, me father! Ya know when I get married and have kids I'll let them all sleep together. In the one bed if they want to.

MICHAEL Look, Mossy, if you had brothers and sisters in the wan bed they'd soon get randy, the boys'd be getting — ya know. It's nature, that's what it is.

MOSSY (*Doubtfully*) Oh, I know, I know, but still and all — ya know? Anyways —

MICHAEL (*Looks at him for a moment*) Ye're gas, Mossy, ya know that? Ye're just gas. I can't believe what ya done. Changing an exam paper! Christ!

MOSSY (*Up*) Course, if I did have children I'd make them do what was right. (*Down*) Only thing is I don't know meself what's right half the time, so I don't.

MICHAEL From now till summer I'm going to sleep in me pelt, so I am.

He lies back and closes his eyes with MOSSY *staring at him. Lights down on the boys and up on the three girls who are now sitting in a group.*

TESS Arragh look at ya, Mon, the way yer plaits have all come out!

MONICA It's driving me bats, me hair. Course I can't have short hair like you, Tess. Oh, no siree! Certainly not! And I can't have a fringe like Winnie there! No, it has to be long and flowing. *Flowing!* Just to keep me two aunties happy. The aggravation of it!

WINNIE Tomorrow during Religion class I'll come behind ya with a big scissors and go snip-snip, snip-snip!

MONICA That's not funny, Winnie, so it's not! If anything like that happened I'd be walloped.

WINNIE (*Pause*) Does he really bate ya, Mon?

MONICA Yeah.

WINNIE (*Pause*) What does he hit ya with? Is it his belt? Or a switch?

MONICA Oh, what does it matter what he hits me with?

She bursts into tears and TESS *holds her while*
WINNIE *watches, mouth open.*

TESS   It's all right, Mon, 's all right.

MONICA (*Through tears*) He says I'm a slut. Me Mammy
thinks that as well. I just know it. One day, me
Mammy says, one day ya'll learn yer lesson,
child. What d'ya think she meant be that,
Winnie?

WINNIE Why didn't ya ask her? Straight out? I would've,
in your shoes.

*The other two look at her. Lights down on the
girls and up on the boys as before, both lying
back, eyes closed.*

MOSSY   Did ya ever, Michael — ? Ya know? Hold yer
— in yer hand?

MICHAEL Hold what?

MOSSY   (*Embarrassed*) Ya know —

MICHAEL (*Pointing to his crotch*) Ya mean me — member?

MOSSY   (*Looking away*) Yeah.

MICHAEL Course I have.

MOSSY   Me, too.

MICHAEL Go 'way. (*Casually*) I've been at it for years now.

MOSSY   And tell us, Michael, d'ya dream? When it's
pouring out of ya, like? D'ya dream about
things?

MICHAEL Naw. I just use an old facecloth.

MOSSY   I dream. Sometimes it's just white legs. Climb-
ing or getting up and over something. Just
white legs. Nothing else, like. Legs, just.

MICHAEL D'ya know, the Gawks Sullivan dreams about
his mother when he's doing it.

MOSSY   Arragh, for God's sake, go on outta that. His
mother!

MICHAEL That's what he says, anyways. The Gawks.

MOSSY   Makes me feel terrible afterwards, though. What
about you, Michael?

MICHAEL Naw. I feel great.

MOSSY There's something up with me for sure. D'ya know something? I wish I wasn't meself.

MICHAEL *looks at him and the lights come down on them and up on the three girls, all gripped by Monica's story, in full flight.*

MONICA — I had a tantrum. Then he came in! Rip! All the back of me dress. Torn in shreds. That night they made me sleep in a sack from the Farmer's Store.

TESS In a wha'?

WINNIE Am I hearin' this right? They made ya — ?

MONICA Yeah. (*Weeps again*)

TESS Ah, Mon!

WINNIE Were ya in yer nightie? For bed?

MONICA In a sack! In a sack! They said it was — mortification of the flesh —

WINNIE This is beyond the beyond and no mistake.

TESS God Almighty, I'd die if I was put into a sack, so I would!

WINNIE And did they tie it up? The sack?

MONICA 'Tis tied at yer chin.

WINNIE And then he wallops ya?

MONICA No, he only wallops me for something special.

WINNIE Where does he hit ya, Mon? What part of yer body does he hit ya on?

MONICA Ye're too nosy altogether, Winnie Butler, so y'are. The worst thing of all is that I know he likes hurting me.

WINNIE How so?

MONICA The look on his face.

WINNIE (*Pause*) When I have children I'm going to let them grow wild as weeds. No one bothers with weeds and still they grow and they grow —

TESS When I have babies I'll put them all in pink satin, pink satin suits and dresses, pink satin hats and coats. No — wait a minute — they'll

	have to have white shoes and socks. And they'll all walk in front of me in a line and I'll be a big fat goose!
WINNIE	Aren't ya very sure ya'll have babies?
TESS	Sure I'm sure.
WINNIE	My auntie Mary never had any.
TESS	Tha's because she's not married, ya omadawn!
MONICA	What about you, Winnie? What'd ya like to have? Boys or girls?
WINNIE	Oh, give me boys any day of the week!
TESS	Same for me!
MONICA	Me, too!
TESS	Girls is no good.
MONICA	Oh, I wish I was a boy!
WINNIE	Oh, hold yer horses, now. Wouldn't go that far, so I wouldn't. I like being a girl.
MONICA	Ye're talkin' through yer hat, Winnie Butler.
WINNIE	(*Playing adult*) My dear innocent child, there's no comparison being loved by a boy and being loved by a girl. A boy is best.
TESS	D'ya mean to say that our Angela gets more from being loved by Jimmy Moran than he does from being loved by her? Oh, Lord!
WINNIE	Course I do. Jimmy is over the moon with his job in the council offices — but Angela! Angela is in seventh heaven just because he loves her. Such ecstasy!
MONICA	Ecstasy me eye!
WINNIE	I'm sorry ya can't see it, dear, dear child!
MONICA	Ye're so full of yerself, Winnie Butler!

In answer WINNIE *does a kind of twirling dance by herself and the other two watch. Lights down on them and up on the two boys at the other side of the stage.*

MICHAEL	Answer me straight out, Mossy. D'ya know how — females — have children?
MOSSY	Sure how'd I know?

MICHAEL That's the limit!

MOSSY Don't tell the other lads on me, Michael!

MICHAEL Why would I tell such a thing? Sure I'm only interested in spreading knowledge.

Lights down on them, going out on Michael's face. Lights on the girls as before.

TESS Come here to me, though! Doesn't he have a fine head of hair on his shoulders, that fella Michael Grainger!

MONICA He walks like a disciple outta the Bible but he's still a swank.

TESS I hate that feckin' Bible.

MONICA Tess!

WINNIE I believe he's third in his class.

TESS Wan of the priests outta the college told Mammy that Michael Grainger could be first in his class if he'd only put his mind to it.

MONICA Why's he so posh? Is it just because they have all that money? I'd take his pal first, any day of the week.

TESS D'ya mean that Mossy Lannigan? Lord save us, that fella has sheep's eyes.

MONICA Don't care. He talks to people and isn't wan bit stuck-up. Not like yer man Michael Grainger.

TESS D'ya know he gave me chocolate sweets after last year's sports day, the same Mossy Lannigan! They were all mashed up in a ball. He said they got soft in his pocket. Such an eejit!

MONICA What do you think, Winnie?

WINNIE 'Bout what?

MONICA 'Bout Michael Grainger.

WINNIE He said something terrible to me, Michael Grainger. It was so terrible — I shouldn't be saying it now but he said I could broadcast it to the whole wide world for all he cared. He said he didn't believe in anything at all. God or

Heaven or Hell or anything. He said there was nothing out there in the sky. Just all empty. I felt this icy coldness come into me when he said that. I felt I was frozen stiff even though the sun was still shining up there in the heavens!

The other two girls stare at her as the lights come slowly down on the three of them, lastly on Winnie's face. Lights up on the two boys as before.

MOSSY   Michael — (*Pause*) Would you write it out for me?

MICHAEL   Write out what?

MOSSY   Ah, ya know? Men and women. That class a' thing. Just write it out. Then I could read it when I'm on me own.

MICHAEL   Course I will. I'll do drawings as well for ya.

MOSSY   OK. (*Long pause*) Michael?

MICHAEL   Yeah.

MOSSY   How did ya get to be such a Mr Knowall?

MICHAEL   Books mostly. About evolution and stuff. It's made me into an atheist.

MOSSY   Jays! Ya'd better not tell anywan that. Ya could be thrown outta college, so ya could. Tell us. Have ya, ya know? Ever seen a girl?

MICHAEL   Ya mean without a stitch?

MOSSY   Yeah.

MICHAEL   Yeah. What about you?

MOSSY   Wance only.

MICHAEL   You won't need drawings so!

MOSSY   'Twas dark. 'Twas behind the Duffy circus caravan. A lot of the lads were there.

MICHAEL   Oh, I heard about that.

MOSSY   She was wan of the wans outta the circus. (*Pause*) She charged us all tuppence each. For to look.

MICHAEL   Go 'way! And did ya get to touch?

MOSSY   She was the other side of the barrier from us.

MOSSY *suddenly jumps up nervously. Gets on the bicycle and begins to cycle off.*

MICHAEL   Hey! Mossy! Hold on a sec!
MOSSY   Cheerio, so, Michael!
MICHAEL   But where ya goin'?
MOSSY   Hafta go to Confession.

MOSSY *has gone.*

MICHAEL   Confession? Cripes! That fella's the limit and no mistake.

He looks off after MOSSY, *shakes his head, gets on his bike and cycles off. Lights up on the three girls as before.* TESS *points off.*

TESS   Look who's comin' beyond!
MONICA   (*Looking*) God, I can't stand the sight of that wan.
WINNIE   (*Out of a daze*) Who?
TESS   'Tis Vivie Hackett.
MONICA   Daddy says she's a dirty — and I won't use the second word.
TESS   She's always dolled up.
MONICA   Daddy says she should go back to England with her mother and father where they belong!
WINNIE   What're ya talkin' about? Aren't they from the town like the rest of us?
MONICA   Daddy says it's a disgrace what goes on in them council cottages below in Piper's Lane. He says they should be all driven outta the town, that crowd.
WINNIE   Wonder what 'twould be like? To live in another country?

VIVIE *is pretty, flashy and clearly more developed than the other three, perhaps a year older as well. Slight English accent.*

VIVIE Hello! Are you lot going up the river?

MONICA What if we are?

TESS Aw, Mon!

VIVIE Oh, dearie me! It's like that, is it?

TESS We might be goin' up the river, mightn't we, Winnie? (WINNIE *shrugs*)

VIVIE Thought I might — tag along with you — if you don't mind, that is —

MONICA (*Moving off*) Well, I'm going somewhere else, so I am. (*She moves away*) Tess! (*Louder*) Tess! Are ya comin' or stayin'?

TESS (*Reluctant*) Oh, all right so!

She follows MONICA *off but takes a look back as she does.* VIVIE *and* WINNIE *look at one another.*

WINNIE What's it like? England?

VIVIE You know, I don't give a damn what people say about me.

WINNIE (*Blurts out*) They say yer mother and father believe in nothing! Is that true?

VIVIE They believe in me.

WINNIE Is it true? He paints pictures? Your father? Of naked women?

VIVIE You ask a lot of questions, don't you? (*Pause*) The bombing was terrible. We were all scrunched up in a shelter out back. Sometimes the lights went out. People lit candles. Some said prayers. Some cried. Or shouted out names. Men's names mostly. Off fighting, I suppose.

WINNIE And were ya frightened at all?

VIVIE Of course. But you know something? I felt — alive! That's all that matters, isn't it? To feel alive! You'd like to have your picture painted, wouldn't you?

WINNIE Oh, I couldn't go near your place, aren't ye the talk of the town!

VIVIE (*Laughs*) Is that a fact, now. Do you remember? When we were all small? We spent a summer here. And we all played Cowboys and Indians. It was organized by that boy, Michael Grainger. I remember, I had a tomahawk. Do you remember?

WINNIE We all thought you were swank.

VIVIE Swank! God, if you only knew!

WINNIE Can I ask you something?

VIVIE Gosh, you do ask questions, don't you? OK. What is it?

WINNIE Have ya ever — ya know — ever been with a boy? No! Don't answer! I don't want to hear!

She quickly turns on her heel and rushes away before a startled VIVIE *can do anything.*

VIVIE Hey! Come on back! (*Voice down, shrugs*) What a place!

She looks off after WINNIE *as the lights come down on her.*
Loud tolling of a church bell from the darkness. Evening light up on the upper level. Grounds of the school. The CANON, *a portly, elderly cleric, and* FR JOSEPH *are having a stroll after supper.*

CANON I see, Fr Joseph, I see. And did he? Do what you asked him to do, this boy, Mossy Lannigan?

FR JOSEPH He did, Canon.

CANON And d'ya not think, Fr Joseph, that that might be, well, not to put a tooth in it, that it might be an abuse of the sacrament of Confession?

FR JOSEPH Not at all, Canon. I just told him in the confessional that he'd have to repeat what he said but outside the confession box.

CANON Why?

FR JOSEPH If he wasn't willing to do that I couldn't give him absolution, you see. He had to own up for what he'd done, first. Firm purpose of amendment, Canon.

CANON   Oh, indeed, indeed. So, let me get this right. He owned up, outside the confessional, that he'd stolen into the room and changed the paper of his mock exam — Physics, was it?

FR JOSEPH   Maths. Calculus.

CANON   That'd be Fr Jimmy. Have you told Fr Jimmy all this?

FR JOSEPH   I thought I should discuss it with you first, Canon. It being so serious, like.

CANON   Oh, very serious, very serious, yes-yes.

FR JOSEPH   There's more, Canon.

CANON   What more?

FR JOSEPH   (*Deep breath*) There's filth in this college!

CANON   What sort of filth, Father?

FR JOSEPH   Bodily filth!

CANON   Bodily filth. (*Slow pause*) You know it's a strange habit the way boys give everyone nicknames. Have you ever thought about that, Fr Joseph?

FR JOSEPH   No, Canon. What I mean is it doesn't concern me.

CANON   Think about it, Father. It's a kind of mockery, don't you know. Pulling people down a peg or two. They call me Big Dog.

> FR JOSEPH *tries to say something at this but the* CANON *raises his hand. He is not to be interrupted.*

Oh, yes! I know it well, I do, I do. Ears listening. Mossy Lannigan. A day-boy? Right? Father's in the army?

FR JOSEPH   The very one.

CANON   That father of his will have a fit. Not a nice man, that father. Dangerous.

FR JOSEPH   The boy will have to be made an example of! Before the whole school.

CANON   They call Fr Jimmy The Spirit Lamp. Science and so on. Somehow I think there's more to it than that though. Spirit Lamp. Yes-yes-yes —

FR JOSEPH	Canon —
CANON	And they call poor Fr Seamus Stutters. Very cruel, don't you think? Stutters? Just because God has given the poor man a speech impediment.
FR JOSEPH	But what about the filth, Canon? The filth!
CANON	'Tis like they have a whole language of their own. Boys. And they call you Fishy, Fr Joseph.
FR JOSEPH	I know that, Canon.
CANON	Mossy Lannigan. I always thought him a harmless enough creature. Big Dog. I've spent a long time trying to work that one out. And, do you know something? I've become attached to it, so I have. Big Dog. What about yourself, Fr Joseph? Does it bother you being called Fishy behind your back?
FR JOSEPH	They'd never use the expression to my face, Canon.
CANON	Now, tell us, what are we going to do with a boy who sneaks into a priest's room and changes his exam paper? Hmm?

They stroll off together. Lights down.
Night scene. Sounds of a river in full flow. Sounds go down as lights come up but sound of running water runs underneath the following scene. WINNIE *is downstage at the edge of the stage looking out over the river* (audience). MICHAEL *lounges behind her, watching her.*

WINNIE	(*Nervously*) I just love the river in the nighttime. Don't you, Michael?
MICHAEL	Yeah.

MICHAEL *mimes throwing a stone into the river. Both watch and wait expectantly. The sound of a stone — plop! — falling into deep water.*

WINNIE	The water looks so — invitin', like —

MICHAEL Can't ya come and sit down beside me?

She moves closer but kneels a little apart from him, still looking out over the river.

WINNIE 'Tis our own special place, this. Isn't it, Michael? The Gash. Why do they call it The Gash?

MICHAEL It's the white water out there over the rocks at the fork in the river. Gowlawn Gash.

WINNIE And is it true everything outta the town ends up in that swally hole beyond there?

MICHAEL That's only auld talk.

WINNIE Monica says her father said they dragged it wance for a man's body that was drowned offa the bridge.

MICHAEL Don't be thinking them things.

WINNIE I hafta think of them things. I can't help meself, so I can't. Did ya really mean it? What ya said before? That we could go off someplace foreign together?

MICHAEL Course I did. Greece, maybe. And would you come with me?

WINNIE The only thing stopping me is Mam. She'd be lost without me.

MICHAEL Not many girls would be ready to do that. Go off, I mean.

WINNIE Don't ya know an awful lot about girls!

He laughs, shaking his head. Then she laughs with him. Then another awkward pause.

MICHAEL I love coming down the river at night. Ya know, I come down here to get away.

WINNIE Away from what?

MICHAEL Me mother and father, mostly. There are times that my head is bursting with everything that's in it. Then I have to go off on me own. To think things out.

WINNIE What class a' things? In yer head?

MICHAEL	Different things. Where badness comes from, for instance.
WINNIE	You're an oddity 'n no mistake. Maybe it's because you're an only child. 'Tisn't right to be on yer own all the time.
MICHAEL	Tell us. Is it true you work for the old people? Is it? Housekeeping — shopping?
WINNIE	Don't want to talk about it —
MICHAEL	But is it true?
WINNIE	I took a vow —
MICHAEL	A what?
WINNIE	A vow, a vow. Like the nuns. To keep it a secret. That way it'd be — works a' charity. And now you know about it. Not fair so it's not!
MICHAEL	But sure lots of people know you do it. But what I want to know is: don't ya get disgusted? They smell something fierce, auld wans.
WINNIE	Who else knows 'cept you? Even me Mam doesn't know!
MICHAEL	But doesn't it make ya vomit? Cleanin' for them in the bed?
WINNIE	Oh, lave me alone, Michael Grainger, lave me alone!
MICHAEL	Sorry. Didn't mean to —
WINNIE	It might give you a bit of pleasure if you thought of someone else for a change! 'Stead of just yerself!
MICHAEL	That could be true. But, ya know something? I think that behind your back you're just laughing at it all.
WINNIE	What do ya mean?
MICHAEL	I seen the look on yer face. Shaking your curls and grinning at everything.
WINNIE	'Tis true. I find most things ridiculous entirely.
MICHAEL	Me too.
WINNIE	If ya can't laugh at it what hope is there?
MICHAEL	(*Excitedly*) You know you're dead right! You know something? It'd be wild if we could see what was down in that swally hole beyond. If

it suddenly threw up everything in a gush, like the geysers in Iceland, prams and bed springs, Ma Healy's chamber pot, and Biker Coady's old bikes, bones and saucepans and somebody's nightshirt . . .

> WINNIE *jumps up with a laugh. She does one of her twirls about while* MICHAEL *watches her. Then she goes and picks up a stick from nearby. She looks at him, testing the switch in her hand — swish, swish — while he looks on with a kind of shocked fascination.*

WINNIE You know, when I laugh at them all I think I'm going to be punished for it. Everybody says you're a swank because ye have pots of money 'n live in a big house.

MICHAEL I never even think about them things.

WINNIE Sometimes I imagine meself a tinker's child. Having to beg, nothing to eat. Then at night-time me father'd wallop me.

> *She tests the switch again in her hand — swish, swish.*

MICHAEL Don't talk like that! Give me that yoke (*the switch, but she holds on to it*).

WINNIE It's what I imagine.

MICHAEL Things don't happen like that.

WINNIE Happens to Monica.

MICHAEL What does?

WINNIE He wallops her. Hard. Her Da.

MICHAEL Don't believe it.

WINNIE Well, ya can.

MICHAEL The guards should stop him. And take Monica away from him.

WINNIE No wan's ever beaten me. Michael?

MICHAEL What?

WINNIE Did ya ever — beat anywan?

MICHAEL Don't be talking that way!
WINNIE With this switch, maybe. Look how sharp it is. (*Demonstrating*) It goes slap, slap!
MICHAEL Here! Give me that!

He grabs the switch from her and throws it away, then watches her as she goes and retrieves it. She hands it back to him.

WINNIE Hit me with it.
MICHAEL What're ya sayin'?
WINNIE On the legs. Go on.
MICHAEL No!
WINNIE I want ya to.
MICHAEL No!

Even as he says this he taps her lightly with the switch.

WINNIE Not that way. On me skin. I want to see what it feels like. Please!
MICHAEL (*Wildly*) I'll teach you please! Say please! Say please!
WINNIE Harder! Until it hurts!
MICHAEL Harder! I'll give you harder, little bitch! You asked for it, didn't you? You asked for it!

He has thrown away the switch and is now striking her with his hands. She cries out and he stops, collapsing into tears. He rushes away, sobbing, head down.

WINNIE Michael! No! Don't go!

Lights down on her face, tear-stained, utterly confused by what has happened.
Lights up on MRS BUTLER working in her kitchen. She looks up as WINNIE walks in, slowly. A pause.

MRS BUTLER Winnie? Are you all right? (WINNIE *nods*) Where've you been till this hour? Wait'll ya hear the news!

WINNIE What news?

MRS BUTLER It's Una! The baby's arrived. 'Tis a girl. Isn't it great?

WINNIE So I'm an auntie once again.

MRS BUTLER Ya make it sound like having consumption. 'Tis delighted you should be, instead of the long face.

WINNIE (*Sarcastic*) Oh, I'm delighted, to be sure. I'm an auntie five times over between all of them, me brothers and me sister, and I still don't know what's going on. Why don't ya tell me things? Why? Why?

MRS BUTLER Oh, now!

WINNIE When the blood first started ya told me to talk to the priest —

MRS BUTLER But I helped ya, Winnie. Didn't I?

WINNIE He told me to pray. He told me to pray for all the women of the world. How could I pray for so many people at the wan time? (*She bursts into tears*)

MRS BUTLER Winnie, Winnie! Come here to me.

WINNIE No-no! I'm not a baby anymore, so I'm not!

MRS BUTLER I know that, dear, I know that.

WINNIE I'm so — so — so confused, so I am.

MRS BUTLER Will I make ya some pancakes?

WINNIE Don't want any pancakes.

MRS BUTLER Your Daddy was a good man when he was alive, Winnie.

WINNIE What has he got to do with anything, me Daddy? I was out with Michael Grainger, that's where I was!

MRS BUTLER What! He's not your class of boy, Winnie.

WINNIE What class a' boy is he, so?

MRS BUTLER Stuck-up. Like all them Graingers.

WINNIE He's not a bit stuck-up! I hate you! I hate you!

MRS BUTLER Winnie. (*Finding the words*) Ya hafta offer up

yer life. All women has to do that. Tha's the
beginning and the end of it.

WINNIE What's the point in saying something like that?
Means nothing.

MRS BUTLER 'S the truth. 'N I don't want ya seeing that
young fella again. D'ya hear me, Winnie? (*No
answer*) Winnie!

WINNIE All right!

MRS BUTLER It's dangerous, so 'tis.

WINNIE What's dangerous?

MRS BUTLER That kind of carry-on.

WINNIE What kind a' carry-on?

MRS BUTLER Ye're far too young to be talking to boys. 'Tisn't
— modest.

WINNIE I feel the strangest things going on inside a' me.

MRS BUTLER God Almighty!

WINNIE Why do I feel like that? It's like — being taken
over. It's like I'm not holding onto anything
anymore —

MRS BUTLER Winnie! I want you to see the priest —

WINNIE I don't want to see a priest!

MRS BUTLER Now, miss, I want no more of that!

WINNIE Why won't ya talk to me?

MRS BUTLER When it's time. I'll talk to ya.

WINNIE What time?

MRS BUTLER When it's time. For ya to get married. Like yer
sister Una.

WINNIE I don't want to get married! I'm not even sixteen!

She runs off, sobbing.

MRS BUTLER What in the name of God has gotten into her?
Winnie!

*Lights down on her, standing there uncertainly.
Lights up on* MOSSY *and* MICHAEL *doing their
homework together in Michael's home.*

MICHAEL Have you finished the Greek trans? There's

twenty-five lines of Homer as well as Thucydides?

MOSSY What use is this Greek? Why do we have to do the frigging stuff? What does it matter to me who won the Peloponnesian War with the whole world collapsing in on top of me.

MICHAEL What's up with you now? (*Pause*) Come on, Mossy, out with it!

MOSSY Why is it ya always know something's wrong with me?

MICHAEL What is it?

MOSSY Fishy.

MICHAEL Fr Joseph? What about him?

MOSSY He knows all about me changing the sums. I'm finished, so I am.

MICHAEL Jaysus! How did that happen?

MOSSY And he found the copybook as well. The one ya wrote for me. 'Member? Men and women and stuff. Where ya drew the pictures of them doing it.

MICHAEL But how'd he get it?

MOSSY He went through me desk. He made me stand there and watch him. 'Twas terrible, so it was.

MICHAEL I see.

MOSSY But I wouldn't tell him 'twas you, Michael. He kept at me for hours. Trying to brainwash me, he was like the bloody Koreans.

MICHAEL (*Worried*) I don't give a shit, so I don't. I don't care. He can do whatever he wants. It doesn't matter to me, boy.

MOSSY No, Father, I says to him. I'm not tellin'. Never!

MICHAEL Ye're wrong about reading Greek, Mossy. I get everything out of reading that stuff. I love reading about ancient Greece. It's like going to a bright place, everything white in that sunshine. And I know there's freedom there no matter what amount of battles go on, killing 'n all. It's the way everything is laid out crystal clear, do you know what I mean? On that page.

What did Fishy say?

MOSSY He said the boy who wrote that stuff was a perverted pup. Sorry, Michael.

MICHAEL One day — one day I'm going to go there. To Greece. To the Mediterranean Sea. To Syracuse and where Troy was and Piraeus, Thermopylae and Delphi. Everywhere.

MOSSY I'd never tell on ya, Michael. Never!

MICHAEL 'N I'm going to walk where those people used to walk. In their footsteps, like.

MOSSY I'll go with ya, Michael! Bedamn but I'll go with ya! I will, so!

> MRS GRAINGER *comes in to the two boys. She is a well turned-out matron of somewhat forbidding manner.*

MRS GRAINGER Isn't it time now for you two gentlemen to put away the books?

MICHAEL Could we have some tea, Mum?

MRS GRAINGER Now, Michael, you know full well that the maid is long gone for the day. It's time to go home, Mossy.

MOSSY Yes, missus. Could I ask a favour, missus?

MRS GRAINGER A favour? What favour?

MOSSY Ah, 'tis nuthin'. I'll be off, so!

MRS GRAINGER No! Finish what you have to say! It's not — seemly to begin something and not finish it. Shows a lack of character, young man.

MOSSY Right so! Ah-mm. (*Deep breath*) Could you loan me the fare, missus, for to go to England? I'd pay it back in a fortnight with a bit of fortune.

MRS GRAINGER England? England! Bless us, what are you talking about, Mossy Lannigan? What about school?

MOSSY Okeydokey, so. Say no more, missus. Forget I ever opened me mouth. I'm off, Michael.

> *He leaves, watched by* MICHAEL *and* MRS GRAINGER.

MRS GRAINGER I wish you wouldn't — consort with that fellow, Michael.

MICHAEL Consort? Consort?

MRS GRAINGER Michael, don't correct me. I'm your mother. I now know I was right when I asked your father to send you to a proper boarding school. The Jesuits or the Benedictines. But, no. (*Bitterly*) He knew better, your father. He always knows better. My son must learn the hard way, as I did. That's what your father said. The hard way, indeed. Mixing with the riff-raff of this town.

MICHAEL (*Yell*) He is my best friend!

MRS GRAINGER (*Yelling back*) Riff-raff!

MICHAEL My best friend!

They stand shaking, glaring at one another. Lights down on them.

Lights up, upstage. Dark shadows. The CANON *and three* PRIESTS *sit behind a table. The dark wall to the side opens up.* FR JOSEPH *stands there with* SHELLY, CAREY *and* LINK *in bright light. They look off into the school assembly, offstage. Noise off of hundreds of boys shuffling, coughing and whispering.* FR JOSEPH *yells 'Silence!' and at once there is silence. He yells 'Sit!' The sounds of hundreds of boys taking their seats behind desks.*

FR JOSEPH You all know why we are here. I intend to wipe out the evil in this college and I will start with these three smoker reprobates!

The three boys line up and he canes them on the hands. He gestures and the boys troop off. The wall closes and FR JOSEPH *walks down to the* PRIESTS *behind the table. He stands there with papers in his hands.*

Here's the next case we have to deal with, Canon. I've brought the filthy pictures, for your perusal.

CANON Hold on a minute, Fr Joseph. (*Prayer*) Almighty God, hear our prayers, grant us the guidance of the Holy Spirit so that we may come to proper judgement in the matter before us.

PRIESTS Amen!

FR JACK Where's that draught coming from? Is it any wonder? Who left that window open?

FR SEAMUS (*Stuttering*) I op-p-p-p-p-pened it! I n-n-n-n-need air!

FR JACK Is it to give us pneumonia? Is that what you're at?

FR SEAMUS Oh, sh-sh-sh-sh-shut it so! If that'll sa-sa-sa-sa-satisfy you!

CANON Now-now-now, lads, some decorum, if you please!

FR JACK Well, I'm not sitting here getting my death of cold!

He jumps up and closes the window with a crash.

FR JOSEPH But what about these filthy pictures, Canon? Confiscated in the study hall!

FR SEAMUS I c-c-c-c-can't breathe, Ca-Ca-Ca-Canon.

CANON You'll be all right, Seamus. Take a deep breath and count to ten, there's a good man. We'll look at this trash.

The PRIESTS gather around to look at the pictures on the table, with the exception of FR SEAMUS who is doing his breathing to one side.

And have the prime buckos involved been chastised, Fr Joseph?

FR JOSEPH Not yet, Canon. I will name them now.

FR KIERAN (*With pictures*) Lord save us, will you look at

this? Look at the naked hussies!

FR JACK   Where could they get this stuff?

FR JOSEPH   Torn out of books mostly.

FR KIERAN   What's the world coming to, I ask you?

FR JOSEPH   There's worse to come!

CANON   Worse?

FR JOSEPH   I've found the very root of this abomination, Canon. (*He hands over Michael's copybook*) Look at it, Canon.

FR KIERAN   What is it, Canon?

CANON   Could a boy have written this? A boy?

FR JACK   What is it? What is it?

FR JOSEPH   It's a book of fornication!

CANON   But a boy? A boy? I cannot credit it!

FR JOSEPH   A depraved scut!

CANON   Where did you get it?

FR JOSEPH   From the day-boy, Mossy Lannigan.

CANON   Mossy Lannigan? Never! He could never write such a thing.

FR JOSEPH   He didn't write it.

CANON   Then who did?

FR JOSEPH   Despite persistent questions young Lannigan wouldn't tell.

> FR SEAMUS *has been looking at the pictures on the table. He holds up one of them.*

FR SEAMUS   Th-th-th-this is — The Judgement of Pa-Pa-Pa-Paris!

FR JACK   What's he going on about now?

FR SEAMUS   L-L-L-L-Lucas C-C-C-Cranach. Th-th-th-the Elder! The grea-grea-great Ger-Ger-German painter!

CANON   Gather up all them pictures and throw them in the fire! This instant!

> FR KIERAN *gathers up the pictures and leaves with them.*

38

FR JOSEPH   You see, I've worked out who wrote in that copybook, Canon.

CANON   (*Ironical*) Is that a fact, Fr Joseph? And how did you do that?

FR JOSEPH   Handwriting. (*Showing more paper*) Compare the two. As plain as plain can be.

CANON   Well? Who is it, so?

FR JOSEPH   Michael Grainger.

FR JACK   (*Disbelief*) Young Grainger!

CANON   You'd better be sure of what you're saying, Father. Making such an accusation.

FR JOSEPH   Sure I'm sure, Canon.

CANON   His father is an important man, not only in this town but beyond. If you're wrong it would be a serious mistake, yes-yes, very serious —

FR JACK   Very serious —

> FR SEAMUS *has risen to his feet, shaking, but at first the others pay no heed to him. He then goes into a kind of spasm and the others are shocked by his behaviour.*

FR SEAMUS   Hypo-hypo-hypo-hypocrites! The lot of us! Whi-whi-whi-whited sepulchres! That's — what-we-are!

CANON   (*Kindly*) Now-now, Seamus —

FR SEAMUS   Who among us is p-p-p-p-pure? Who ca-a-can ca-ca-cast the first stone? Which of us is fi-fi-fi-fit to judge?

CANON   (*Sternly*) Seamus!

> But FR SEAMUS *has become even more frantic. He throws off his soutane and clerical collar, becoming a shivering old man in a ragged white shirt and braces.*

FR SEAMUS   Hi-hi-hi-hiding under the black! Hi-hi-hiding our trans-transgressions, seeeeeecret sins! Off with it! Off with it! The truth! The truth will out!

39

The CANON *goes, picks up the soutane and collar and gently leads him away, watched by the shocked* PRIESTS.

FR JACK What was he talking about?

No answer, and the lights come down on them.
A recording of a 1930s dance tune ('Goodnight, sweetheart, soon we'll meet tomorrow — ') comes wafting out of the darkness.
Lights up on boys arranged in couples by the PREFECT *of the opening of the play. The* PREFECT *is fiddling with the record player. The boys look bored.*

PREFECT Now, lads! Ye're going to have to learn a bit of manners, so ye are. Ye have to learn how to dance to the music before ye leave this place. Take yer partners now. One! Two! Three!

The boys hold one another clumsily and at the prefect's direction they begin to waltz about in a makeshift dance. General embarrassment and tittering.

Stop that sniggering! Listen to the music. Ye're a right pack of bullocks, so ye are!

He conducts them, pushing them into place. A boy runs on and whispers in his ear. The PREFECT *rushes away with the boy, calling back as he goes.*

Keep it up, now, keep it going on yer own! I'll be back!

Immediately the dancing stops, replaced by some rough-house stuff, jostling, shouldering, the odd punch. LINK *has stuffed newspaper under his jersey to make two pendulous breasts.*

LINK Lookit me titties! Lookit me titties!

> *The others shout: 'Jaysus, look at him!' 'Good*
> *man, Link!' 'Go on, Link!'*
> LINK *chases them all away. The music still*
> *plays. A moment's pause. Then two boys waltz*
> *out of the darkness. This is different, two boys*
> *who can clearly dance with one another.* MOSSY
> *appears and watches them. The music dies down*
> *and they kiss. They see* MOSSY *and race away.*
> MOSSY *moves off slowly. Lights down on him.*
> *Lights up on the lower level of the stage and*
> MOSSY *walks quickly into the light, calling out.*

MOSSY Michael! Michael! Michael!

> *He turns:* VIVIE *staggers on, a bottle in one hand.*

VIVIE Lost someone, have you?

MOSSY Ah, I was just — y'know —

VIVIE Christ, I'm wrecked. Wasted.

MOSSY What happened you?

VIVIE Want some cider?

MOSSY Ah, no. I'm a pioneer, don't you know.

VIVIE One of those? Oh, my God, a bloody teetotaller!

MOSSY (*Shame-faced*) Yeah. That's me.

VIVIE Know something? You're a funny one. I like
you. You're not like the rest of them.

MOSSY Ya must be jokin' me!

VIVIE No, I mean it. Really do. No joke.

MOSSY Cripes! That's a good wan, so 'tis. You! Of all
people!

VIVIE What's the problem, then?

MOSSY Nuthin'.

VIVIE You were calling someone just now —

MOSSY Michael. Michael Grainger.

VIVIE (*Slurred, swigging from bottle*) Why'reyoucall-
ing'im?

MOSSY Want to say goodbye to him.

VIVIE   Goodbye? You going somewhere, are you? So am I! Know where I'm going? I'm going to Paris. I'm going to model for all the great painters in their studios! I'm going to be every kind of woman you can think of! I'm going to be a goddess on one of those — whatyoumaycallem — pedestals! I'm going to be a saint! I'm going to be a whore! I'm going to be somebody, I'm going to be a nobody! Anything! Everything you can — think of — Michael Grainger, hmm? You remember the time we all played together? When we were small? Cowboys and Indians. I was the Indian maiden tied to a tree. What a lark! Hah! And Michael Grainger. He was General Custer with a sword. Oh, boy! Can't remember what you were. Do you remember? What you were?

MOSSY   (*Depressed*) Don't remember. Maybe I wasn't there at all.

VIVIE   Oh, you were there. I remember you. Do you have a girlfriend?

MOSSY   Me? Oh, no!

VIVIE   You want to? You know? Mess around. I'm hot.

MOSSY   What? Oh, I don't think so —

VIVIE   If you want to we can go into the bushes. (*Off*) Over there.

MOSSY   Don't think so —

She looks at him for a moment. Then turns on her heel and staggers away.

VIVIE   OK! OK! Forget it! See you later. Alligator! Ta-ta, lover-boy!

He watches her go, talking to himself.

MOSSY   One word! All I had to say was one word. And she'd have let me. One word. Bet Michael would have said 'yes'. What's up with me? Every door is shut on me. Every door shut.

Lights down on him as he wanders off. Lights up on MICHAEL *walking out of the darkness on the other side of the stage. He turns sharply.* WINNIE *is creeping along behind him.*

WINNIE I snuck out when Mammy went to bed. I just knew you'd be down here.

MICHAEL Better for you to go home.

WINNIE Why, so?

MICHAEL You don't want to be next or near the likes of me.

WINNIE What's wrong? Something's wrong with ya?

MICHAEL I'm bad. That's all.

WINNIE Ya can talk to me, Michael —

MICHAEL Go 'way! Leave me alone!

WINNIE No, I'm staying put. First I have to hear ya say what's up with ya. Can't ya tell me?

MICHAEL Why? What's it to do with you?

WINNIE Don't know why, but it means everything to me right now.

MICHAEL Far better off never knowing me, so you would —

WINNIE Tha's not true, Michael — 'n ya know it!

MICHAEL Much better off. I just bring trouble to everyone.

WINNIE Oh, Michael —

She throws her arms about him and holds him firmly. He suddenly kisses her violently.

Do you love me, Michael?

MICHAEL No such thing as love. No such thing.

WINNIE 'Tisn't right to say that!

MICHAEL Lie down.

WINNIE What do you want to do?

MICHAEL Just lie down.

43

She does so and he lies on top of her, fumbling with her clothes and his own.

WINNIE What're ya doin'? Michael!

The CANON and a line of impassive priests, soutanes and birettas, appear, looking out into the audience.
The lights come down on MICHAEL and WINNIE.

(*Screaming*) You're hurting me! You're hurting me!

The lights come down on the line of priests.

ACT TWO

Lights up, downstage. The space is dominated by a large, old-fashioned, locked, double-door wardrobe in a pool of light. MOSSY *stands in front of it, trying to open it with several sets of keys. No success.*

MOSSY   Tck-tck-tck, yes, no. This one? Try this one. Open-open-open, oh for Jays' sake. No feckin' good, so it's not. (*Examining keys*) Wonder where all them keys come from? Don't have that many doors in our house, so we don't. Maybe Daddy just keeps the right keys in his pocket? Keeps everything in his pockets. In his waistcoat, maybe, steal in at night, root around. Oh, Daddy, Daddy, Daddy! No, Daddy! (*Daddy voice*) No son of mine — no son of mine will let me down in front of everyone. Hah! Fuck him, anyways.

(*Shift*) Funny that. I'm no longer frightened of him, couldn't care less about anywan or anything anymore, even that strap Vivie, arragh, she's all right, don't care what any a' them say anymore, so I don't, like a weight lifted offa me chest, it is, able to breathe, in, out, no panic or anything. Sorta free, like as if I'm somebody else entirely and not meself.

(*Pulls out a piece of paper*) Go over the list again. Check everything. Don't leave anything to chance. Put letter for Mammy and the girls near tea cosy where they have to find it. Leave diary for Michael in his desk last thing after he's left study but not before so's he won't see me and want to talk. Ticked off, done. Leave note for Tess, can't remember if I've done that or not, too late now, anyways. Give collection of stamps to Josie next door but pretend it means nothing so he won't 'spect anything. Ticked off. Everything ticked off. Funny how I have no worries anymore. Funny how I feel I could do anything now, anything I ever wanted.

He turns to the doors of the wardrobe again but they won't budge. He turns aside, picks up an iron bar. He puts this between the doors and pushes it carefully. He stops to listen. No sound. He pushes the bar harder. Stops to listen again. Still no sound. He pushes again, more and more desperately. Then, with a creak, he prises open the doors. The interior is like a lit shrine and the boy shrinks before it.

A full army officer's uniform hangs inside, facing out like a disembodied presence. This is achieved by the way the cap is placed above the uniform jacket and the high polished boots and leggings below the ballooning knee-pants. Draped across the uniform is a Sam Browne belt and holster. He reaches for the holster, flaps open the cover and removes the revolver. Pause. He pushes the gun into his chest, bending over. As the lights come down: a single shot.

Lights up on WINNIE *and* MONICA *walking by the river bank,* WINNIE *carrying a bunch of flowers.*

WINNIE   I just love wild flowers. 'Cept they don't last long.

MONICA   What did ya want to talk to me about, Win?

WINNIE   Promise not to tell!

MONICA   Cross me heart and hope to die!

WINNIE   Not even Tess —

MONICA   That wan! Sure she's an awful blabbermouth. Why d'ya think I left her behind just now? Go on! Tell us!

WINNIE I'm going to have a baby.

MONICA *wants to get out of there. She turns away, she turns back. The two girls can't look at one another.*

MONICA Sure, how can that be? Aren't ya the same age as the rest of us? God Almighty! How d'ya know?

WINNIE Mam thought I was run down. She took me in to Dr Sullivan. I wasn't run down at all. Will ya still be me best friend, Mon?

MONICA What're ya going to do?

WINNIE Nuthin'. They're talking of a convent below in Waterford.

MONICA Convent? For to be a nun?

WINNIE No, dummy! For to be hid away. Till it's all over.

MONICA And d'ya feel awful, Win?

WINNIE I feel nuthin' at all.

MONICA Oh, my God, 'tis terrible news!

WINNIE Ya promised not to tell!

MONICA And did they tell ya? What's it going to be like? Havin' it? They say 'tis awful.

WINNIE They told me nuthin'. No wan ever tells me anything. But I'm not going to let it best me. I'll go down fighting, so I will.

MONICA Arragh stop! What're ya talking about? Fighting?

WINNIE 'Member when ya told us about yer Da? Hitting ya? 'Member?

MONICA Yeah.

WINNIE I used to think that was the worst thing that could happen, to be beaten by yer own father. And look at me now! Having a baby.

MONICA I don't want to talk about being hit. Ever again, so I don't.

WINNIE 'Tis better to talk about things. That way it's out in the open. Will ya still be me best friend, Mon?

MONICA What do I have to do?

WINNIE Nuthin'. Just be me best friend.

MONICA (*In tears*) Me father'll murder me when he hears about all this!

WINNIE (*Throwing away the flowers*) I don't know why I bother with them auld flowers. Sure they're dead already. D'ya want to walk back?

MONICA (*Sniffing*) Yeah.

WINNIE Doesn't matter who knows about me. I mean it don't matter to me. It's only Mam. She's always thinking of the neighbours. What'll the neighbours think?, says she. What does it matter what they think?, says I, you are what you are what you are. That's the beginning and end of it. Know what I mean?

MONICA (*More tears*) I could be yer secret best friend!

WINNIE But 'twouldn't be the same, secret, would it now? (*Pause*) I'll tell ya wan thing though for sure. I'll never go near them nuns, so I won't.

MONICA You're hard-hearted so y'are, Winnie Butler!

WINNIE Ya hafta be that way sometimes. Just so's ya can keep goin'.

> *There is a loud scream from* TESS, *off. 'Monica! Monica!' The two girls stand waiting.* TESS *comes running on, breathlessly, in tears, a scrap of paper in her hand.*

TESS Monica! Oh, Winnie! Something terrible's happened! 'Tis Mossy Lannigan! He left me a note! He said I was the only one who ever bothered about him. The only one!

> *The three girls stand still,* TESS, *still weeping, holding out the note.*
> *Then they turn and we follow them back into a funeral scene on the upper level. They take their places to one side, beside* VIVIE.
> *On the other side,* MICHAEL *stands with a group of boys. Both groups look back to where*

FR SEAMUS *presides over Mossy's funeral in a corner of the graveyard. A handful of mourners above the coffin and grave. The boys and girls speak in loud whispers.*

LINK   Stutters'll take the whole feckin' day the way he's going.

CAREY   Hey! Christy! Why're they buryin' him over there in the corner?

SHELLY Why d'ya think, ya eejit? Isn't he after shooting himself?

MICHAEL (*Loudly*) Stop that kind of talk!

They stare at MICHAEL. *Our attention now moves to the three girls.*

TESS   (*Gulp*) He's been buried with the unbaptised babies, God help him!

MONICA Shhh, Tess! You're only making it worse on yourself.

TESS   They might as well put him down in an open field, so they might.

WINNIE It don't matter where ye're buried. Everywan rises on the last day. Even if there's only bits of ya left. When ya rise up ye're all perfect and together again as if nothing had happened to ya. Even if ye're shot dead. Or chopped up or anything.

TESS   Vivie was wan a' the first to see him dead. Weren't ya, Vivie?

The other girls look at VIVIE. *A pause.*

WINNIE Is that a fact? Did ya see him dead? What did it look like?

VIVIE   (*Upset*) I went into the house. I don't know why I went in. I heard the shot. It was as if a big red flower had opened up on the front of his shirt. Then they came and covered him up. Why did

49

he do it? Why?

*She rushes away with the girls looking after her
and our attention is drawn to the boys.*

CAREY   Hey, Michael? What did he have to go and do
that for? Mossy, beyond?

MICHAEL   Don't know.

SHELLY   But you're supposed to be his pal.

CAREY   He was always soft in the head. Me Da says all
the Lannigans were ever like that. Cracked.

SHELLY   You're the wan that's cracked, Carey.

CAREY   Go 'way awr that.

LINK   Look, lads, they're finishing up beyond. Let's
go 'n play backs and forwards!

An outburst from MICHAEL *so that he catches
the attention of everyone, boys, girls, mourners
and priest.*

MICHAEL   There's no God, there never was and never
will be. 'Tis all mumbo-jumbo! What good'll it
do Mossy or any of them in the grave?

Mourners drift away as do the boys, leaving
MICHAEL *alone.* WINNIE *lags behind the two
girls who leave her. For a moment* WINNIE *is
about to go towards* MICHAEL *but she turns and
leaves at the approach of* FR SEAMUS.

FR SEAMUS   A wo-wo-wo-word with you, Michael!

MICHAEL   I have to leave this place, Father! For good!

FR SEAMUS   In time, Michael. In time!

MICHAEL   I killed him!

FR SEAMUS   You did — you did — did — no such thing!

MICHAEL   Oh-yes, I did, Father. Never knew he was so —
frail like that. Mossy. Never thought he could
be broke like that. I thought I was doing good!
Talking to him. Telling him things. I wanted

him to be — free! And now look! They say 'tis good. Knowing things. Understanding things. But for what? 'Stead I was just feeding him poison. Why so? Why would something good destroy him? Why? Where did it come from? The destruction of Mossy? Where?

FR SEAMUS   There's no-no-no-no answer to that, Michael. Oh, they'll tell you th-th-th-that there is. But there isn't.

MICHAEL   D'ya know about Winnie Butler, Father?

FR SEAMUS   I do, Michael.

MICHAEL   The whole place knows. I'm finished, so.

FR SEAMUS   It's an am-m-m-m-amazing world we are born into, Michael. But 'tis also the hou-house of damnation. All we c-c-c-c-can do is tr-tr-tr- (*He stops, then with fierce effort*) Try! Try! And try again!

MICHAEL   What am I to do?

FR SEAMUS   (*Deep breath*) Go to the girl! Tell her that you will — that you will stand by her in love! Through th-th-th-thick and th-th-th-thin! Then so-so-so-something may grow out of all this hell.

> MICHAEL *looks at him. Then he walks away, quickly. Lights down on* FR SEAMUS.
> *Cold, early morning light upstage. The grim wall has opened up to reveal the following:*
> *A shivering line of Industrial School boys, in old nightshirts, with towels around their waists, standing impassively, facing the audience. A* CHRISTIAN BROTHER, *in his full clerical garb, carrying a leather strap, stands on guard, also facing out. These boys are different from the college boys, shaven and bruised heads, black eyes, one or two with dirty bandages. Behind their backs we see three cubicle showers with doors closed. But we can see the water pouring down on those inside. Outside each door, on a peg, is a*

towel. The steam rises in the cold morning light. The CHRISTIAN BROTHER *turns and raps a door with his strap. As he does so one of the boys in the line grabs the testicles of another. There is a brief, silent struggle with suppressed guffaws, immediately stopped when the* BROTHER *turns around again. A naked wet boy comes out of the shower, grabs his towel and runs off.*

The BROTHER *raps one of the waiting boys with the strap. The boy runs to the showers, hangs up his towel and goes in, closing the door.*

The same routine is repeated. This time when the BROTHER *turns to rap on a door, one of the boys has contrived a gigantic erection under his towel to the wild but utterly silent hilarity of the others. Just as the* BROTHER *turns back the boy reveals that the erection is a scrub brush with a long handle and it is at this the angry* BROTHER *looks when he's back in line once more.*

Another boy out of the shower and another boy in. Before this image fades, lights up downstage on MR *and* MRS GRAINGER *and the* CANON. MR GRAINGER's *first speech runs, partly under the image of the showers.*

MR GRAINGER St Joseph's Industrial School is one of the finest institutions in this state. Amn't I right, Canon? The work done by the Brothers is the wonder of the whole country. The young criminals are straightened out. When they're let out again they can do something useful for themselves. And the community is safe from their crimes. Could there be any better job than that, I ask you?

MRS GRAINGER (*Weeping*) I won't hear of it! Won't hear of it! You're not going to put our Michael in there! No!

MR GRAINGER Now, Mary —

MRS GRAINGER No!

MR GRAINGER   What I'm doing I'm doing for his own good!
MRS GRAINGER   Good? Locking him up in that place is good?
                May God forgive you!
MR GRAINGER   My son — my only boy — has been found
                to be — degenerate. I've spent nights awake
                thinking of this. What to do? All I know is self-
                discipline. Is that bad? I pulled myself up by
                the bootstraps to where I am today. How? By
                making myself hard. By steeling myself at
                every turn of the road. By controlling myself
                — By not giving in to weakness —
MRS GRAINGER   But you're not Michael!
MR GRAINGER   I will do anything to save him from himself!
                Anything!
MRS GRAINGER   It will kill him to put him in there. With that
                riff-raff! He's a sensitive boy, Michael.
MR GRAINGER   Sensitive! Sensitive! It is you who have made
                him like he is with your mollycoddling and
                your highfalutin' notions above your station —
MRS GRAINGER   Talk to him again! He's in a terrible state at
                what has happened!
MR GRAINGER   I've talked to him till I was blue in the face! It
                was like talking to a pound of melted butter!
                We're gone beyond talk. What he needs now is
                a good, sharp shock to the system. That'll
                knock the dirt out of him!
MRS GRAINGER   Oh, you — ! You're impossible! Canon! You
                know Michael. You know how delicate he is.
                You know what will happen to him in that
                place —
CANON   Well, I have to say it is a curious way of hand-
                ling the situation, yes-yes. Putting the boy away
                like this.
MR GRAINGER   Curious? And what do you mean by that,
                Canon?
CANON   Well, in a case like this we'd normally think
                of a retreat for the boy, a period of reflection
                and silence — in the college — or below in the
                monastery —

MR GRAINGER	Your college has failed our boy!
CANON	And what is that supposed to mean, if I may ask?
MR GRAINGER	I mean where did all that filth come from? In the first place? Not from our home.
CANON	Oh, well, now —
MR GRAINGER	The college has failed our boy. And the bishop agrees with me.
CANON	Well, well. You were talking to the bishop?
MR GRAINGER	He hasn't been in touch with you yet?
CANON	No, he hasn't been in touch with me.
MRS GRAINGER	But what about Michael?
MR GRAINGER	Mary. Listen to me. It'll only be for a few weeks. But our prime boy won't know this. He'll think he's there for the duration. That way the thing will be sorted out before you know it. He'll be back a changed boyo. And nothing will come out into the open. Think of that. No scandal for anyone. Ourselves, the college. The boy himself. He'll go on without a stain. I know how important this is. No scandal waiting to jump out and get you when you make your moves.
CANON	Well, if it is a very temporary measure it might do some good —
MR GRAINGER	Course it will, Canon. I've spoken with the Brothers. They know the ropes. And I've had a word with the District Judge. Everything above board. It will be like what they call a Voluntary Committal.
MRS GRAINGER	I can't believe this —
MR GRAINGER	A quick dose of medicine —
CANON	And the Brothers are most responsible — Yes-yes. Contact with boys less privileged than himself. That could be salutary.
MR GRAINGER	Privilege has nothing to do with it, Canon.
CANON	No-no, I didn't mean —
MRS GRAINGER	But what about the Butler girl?
MR GRAINGER	The who?

MRS GRAINGER The girl —
MR GRAINGER What girl?
MRS GRAINGER The girl who is — in the family way —
MR GRAINGER Don't you worry about that. Money will take care of that.

MRS GRAINGER turns and leaves.

Where're you going?
MRS GRAINGER I'm going to Michael!

GRAINGER and the CANON watch her leave.

MR GRAINGER I blame the Hitler war, Canon. Nothing will ever be the same again after that war. Mr De Valera may have protected this country and kept the war from our shores. Still! The devil is out! Breakdown. Once upon a time everything was in its place. Not anymore. Look at the filth in the picture-houses! Foreign influences! We may not have been invaded before. But we're being invaded now!

Lights down on the two men.
    Lights up on the Butler kitchen as in the opening of the play. A pregnant WINNIE in her slip. MRS BUTLER is now trying out another dress on her.

MRS BUTLER I just let it out here a bit in the front and put these two patches in the sides. Isn't that grand?
WINNIE 'Tis like a tent, so 'tis.
MRS BUTLER Shush, Winnie. Sure 'tis only for a few months more.
WINNIE 'N what'll happen after?
MRS BUTLER 'Tis all provided for.
WINNIE No wan'll look me straight in the face ever again. (*Lifting the dress*) Everybody knows anyways so why bother covering me up? (MRS

BUTLER, *very upset, turns aside*) I'm sorry, Mammy, 'bout everything.

MRS BUTLER I only wish yer Daddy was alive today. That's all.

WINNIE And would he be mad at me?

MRS BUTLER Mad at you? What're ya talking about? Wouldn't he stand up for ya, Winnie? Ways that I can't.

WINNIE What d'ya mean?

MRS BUTLER No wan'd talk about ya behind yer back if yer Daddy was alive. I guarantee ya that. The gossips.

WINNIE Sure I don't care what anywan says about me. Sticks 'n stones.

MRS BUTLER That's what himself would say if he was alive. Ye're the living spit of him! There! (*Dress*) Turn around and let me look at ya!

WINNIE What'd ya mean before? When ya said everything was provided for?

MRS BUTLER You don't have to worry your head about things like that.

WINNIE But I want to know.

MRS BUTLER The nuns'll take good care of ya.

WINNIE I don't want to hear about them nuns again! Ye're hiding something from me!

MRS BUTLER I'm not!

WINNIE Y'are!

MRS BUTLER Why do you want to bother with stuff like that? Haven't ya enough on yer plate?

WINNIE Because it's me! It's me in the middle of it all! Me! No wan else. I have to know everything!

MRS BUTLER (*Decides to tell*) It's all arranged. The doctor 'n everything. The — baby. Afterwards. Everything's settled and paid for.

WINNI Paid for? Money? What money?

MRS BUTLER I can't be tellin' ya them things —

WINNIE But ya hafta!

MRS BUTLER The dress looks great, so it does —

WINNIE (*Wildly*) I have to know! I have to know!

MRS BUTLER	The Graingers.
WINNIE	The Graingers what?
MRS BUTLER	Paid for everything —
WINNIE	(*Sitting down, weakly*) Michael —
MRS BUTLER	Don't even mention that fella's name — ever again! Ever!
WINNIE	(*Almost to herself*) That's why he never got in touch with me. Money.
MRS BUTLER	They've put him away for good.
WINNIE	Put him away where?
MRS BUTLER	Into St Joseph's.
WINNIE	God Almighty! St Joseph's! That place!
MRS BUTLER	Anyways. Isn't it only right that they pay up?
WINNIE	(*Weeping*) They've put a price on me! They've put a price on me!

> *As the lights come down on them* MRS BUTLER *can only look at her, helplessly.*
>
> *Lights up, above. A line of cropped boys face out, with* MICHAEL *at the end of the line. Industrial School clothing. A* CHRISTIAN BROTHER *parades before them. The large wall has now become a tower connecting upper and lower stage levels.*

BROTHER	Right, Mahon! Rule Number One?
MAHON	Rule Number One: To honour and obey the Brother-in-charge. No matter who he is.
BROTHER	Next! O'Neill. Rule Number Two?
O'NEILL	Say to yourself every hour of every day, you're here because you're — because you're a — nobody.
BROTHER	You, Shea. Rule Number Three!
SHEA	Rule Number Three: The only way ya can get outta here — (*Mutter-mutter*)
BROTHER	Yes-yes. Can't hear you!
SHEA	(*Loud yell*) The only way ya can get outta here is by becoming a somebody.
BROTHER	Aha! A somebody! And how do we become a

somebody? Bulger?

BULGER Yes, sir!

BROTHER Yes, Brother!

BULGER Yes, Brother.

BROTHER Well? Go on! Go on! Yes-Brother-what?

BULGER I forget, Brother.

BROTHER You forget, Brother, you forget, do you? (*He beats the boy about the head*) Forget, do you? You stupid clown! Tell him! You! New boy! Grainger!

MICHAEL You become somebody by learning to obey the laws of the Catholic Church and the laws of the state of Ireland, by learning how to work and by earning the respect of your betters —

BROTHER There's one more, Grainger —

MICHAEL And by always trying to be pure in both mind and body.

BROTHER Pure in mind and body. That's the one for you, Grainger. You're learning, Grainger. Were you listening, Bulger?

BULGER Yes, Brother.

BROTHER And now you know it all by heart?

BULGER (*Very distressed*) Can't remember, can't remember —

BROTHER Come here the two of ye — Bulger and Grainger — (*The two boys step forward*) Now the next time I see the two of ye — you, Grainger, will have taught this lunk-head the rules. D'ye hear?

> *All the boys watch as the* CHRISTIAN BROTHER *departs,* MICHAEL *and* BULGER *at a little distance from the others.*

MAHON Rule Number wan, Ratser?

O'NEILL Can't remember, Brother.

MAHON Can't remember me arse, ya little bollix! Tell him, Blade.

SHEA Fuck the Brother-in-charge, the shite.

The boys find this hilarious and there is much rolling about and rough shoving and roaring.

BULGER 'Tis no use. I can't keep anything in me head.
MICHAEL I'll help you.
BULGER 'Tis like as if there's something wrong with me head.
MICHAEL I'll write it out for you.
BULGER No use. Can't read words on paper either.
MAHON How d'ya become somebody? You, Blade!
SHEA Be lifting every fuckin' thing that's not nailed down!

The boys shout out their favorite outrages: 'By getting the whores in a corner', 'By riding them all', 'By breaking into the bank', 'By taking over the whole fuckin' place'. MAHON *stops all this by raising an arm and pointing at* MICHAEL.

MAHON Hey! You-boy! What're you in for?
O'NEILL Will we slit him, Gouger?
MAHON No, Blade. First we'll hear what he has to say. Then we'll slit him!
BULGER (*To* MICHAEL) Ya'd better do as they say. Otherwise they'll do something terrible to ya.

MAHON *takes out a penknife, opens it and leads the other boys, menacingly, towards* MICHAEL. *Then one of the other boys, who has been looking off, shouts a warning to the others: 'Nix! Nix!' and the whole group freezes as a young* CHRISTIAN BROTHER *comes on with a parcel. He hands the parcel to* MICHAEL.

2ND BROTHER Your mother left it in for you.

The BROTHER *departs and* MICHAEL *looks at the ring of boys. He offers the parcel to* MAHON.

MICHAEL Here. Take it. Share it out.

> MAHON *grabs the parcel and the group of boys tear it open like animals. It contains various items of food and they devour everything as they rush away.* MICHAEL *turns away from the sight towards* BULGER.

Does anyone ever escape out of here?
BULGER All the time. But they're always brought back again be the guards.
MICHAEL What way do they escape?
BULGER Be crossing the roofs to the outside wall. Then there's a forty-foot drop.
MICHAEL But how do ya get down?
BULGER That's up to you.
MICHAEL What if ya went the other way?
BULGER Towards the tower?
MICHAEL Right.
BULGER Sure that'd be mad. That tower is terrible high altogether. Sure there's no way down from that.

> MICHAEL *says nothing. He walks away as* BULGER *looks after him.* MAHON *leads* O'NEILL *and* SHEA *back on. They're carrying hurley sticks and surround* BULGER.

MAHON What were ye talkin'about? Just now? You and yer man?

> BULGER *is boxed in between the boys.*

BULGER Nuthin' —
MAHON Answer me, ya fucker!

> *Very quick: he strikes* BULGER *about the ankles with the hurley and it hurts. The other boys join in, hitting* BULGER *as if he were a ball between them.* BULGER *screams and falls. One or two raise*

hurleys and strike the screaming boy on the ground.

MAHON Stoppit! Don't kill the cunt!

They all rush away and MICHAEL *rushes on from another direction. He bends and lifts* BULGER, *who is bleeding from his head, to his feet.*

BULGER My head, my head!
MICHAEL Get ya help —

He lifts BULGER *who is bleading heavily and they stagger away.* BULGER *stops.*

BULGER Michael — run away — run away from here —

MICHAEL *helps him off and the lights come down on them.*
   Lights up on WINNIE *in the darkness by the river bank. She is already in labour, groaning and breathing heavily. For a moment she stands, holding up an old towel and a scissors. She tries to settle herself on the ground, with difficulty, shifting about from position to position. Finally she lies down, her back to the audience, and removes her underwear. She gives birth with a single scream and holds up a bloody foetus. She cuts the cord and collapses back, the dead foetus in her arms.*

WINNIE Michael! Michael! Cold — it's so cold — so cold —

Lights up on the dormitory of the Industrial School. Boys in striped pyjamas, sitting and lying about on the beds chatting, watched by the CHRISTIAN BROTHER. MICHAEL *walks on distractedly and stands aside.*

2ND BROTHER (*To* MICHAEL) How's Bulger? (*No response from* MICHAEL) Ya can't be of any more help to him, Grainger. You should be in bed. It's lights out. You'll only get into more trouble. (*He turns away to go, but returns*) Did no one say anything to you?

MICHAEL About what, Brother?

2ND BROTHER About that girl.

MICHAEL Is it Winnie Butler?

2ND BROTHER That's her name. I shouldn't be talking to you like this at all, so I shouldn't.

MICHAEL What happened her?

2ND BROTHER She died. Down by the river, they say.

MICHAEL (*Grief*) Winnie! (*Long pause*) Dead! Was she — drowned?

2ND BROTHER No. Just on the bank of the river. They found her.

MICHAEL I know the place. It's called Gowlawn Gash. Winnie — Winnie —

2ND BROTHER I'm sorry. To be telling you all this.

MICHAEL I was only ever thinking of myself. I never thought, really thought, about Mossy and Winnie. Never. Only myself. And now I think of them day and night. But it's too late.

2ND BROTHER (*As he leaves*) Pray for her, Grainger, pray for her immortal soul.

MICHAEL (*Alone, a manic, derisive yell*) Pray? Pray? Hah!

He turns to watch the other boys in the dormitory but he still remains apart. The boys have gathered around in a circle, with MAHON *central.*

MAHON (*Holding up the coin*) Here's the half-crown. Whoever hits it first gets to keep it.

He puts the coin in the centre of the circle. As they speak, all the boys manipulate themselves, the idea being to hit the coin as they masturbate. Various grunting and groaning sounds as they get erections. Shouts of: 'I'm up! I'm up!'

O'NEILL Where'd ya get the half-crown, Gouger.

MAHON Where the fuck d'ya think?

SHEA He stole it outta the box in the chapel.

MAHON Shag off, Blade!

SHEA I am shagging off — Huh! Huh! Huh!

> MICHAEL *turns away from the scene and at once the lights come down on the boys. He puts on a jacket, furtively. He picks up a rag, grabs a small sack and slings it over his shoulder and walks towards the tower, examining it.*

MICHAEL They'll expect me to go the other way. Never again in my life will I do what they expect me to! Never!

> *He climbs down the side of the tower, to the lower stage, falling the last few feet and disappearing from view. The front of the ramp slowly opens up. The effect is of a dark cave or tunnel opening up.* MICHAEL *appears within and staggers forward downstage into light. He is injured and bedraggled.*
>
> *Behind him walks the figure of a white-faced* WINNIE *in a simple dress. She remains some distance behind him, looking at him. She finds a place to one side, never taking her eyes off him from now until the end of the play.*
>
> *A cry of* MOSSY *from within the tunnel, calling out 'Michael! Michael!'* MICHAEL *stiffens, alert, but doesn't look back. The bloodied figure of* MOSSY *is in the tunnel behind him, his hand out.*

MOSSY Michael! Give me your hand, Michael! Just your hand.

MICHAEL Where am I? What's happening to me?

MOSSY You're passing through, Michael.

MICHAEL (*Cry*) You're not Mossy Lannigan, whatever you are. Isn't he dead and buried!

He turns away as if to leave. Then stops.

MOSSY   Don't go, Michael. Take me hand. Just me finger, is all.

MICHAEL   (*Out*) I crossed the roofs to the tower. It was pitch black. I grabbed the lightning conductor with a rag and started down. Suddenly I could see the road beyond going off into the distance —

MOSSY   We're still best pals, aren't we, Michael?

MICHAEL   But you're dead. I'm alive. If ya make that road, I said to meself, you'll be free.

MOSSY   That's all ya have to do, is take me hand.

MICHAEL   (*Out*) Then I saw lights in the distance. There's no going back now, says I. It has to be straight ahead or nothing. Then I fell. I don't remember anything else.

MOSSY   If I hold yer hand ya can come with me — Dying is easy, so 'tis.

MICHAEL   (*Low*) Where do you be now, Mossy?

MOSSY   Us. There's a lot of us. We're everywhere and nowhere, so we are. Sometimes we sit perched on steeples or in the corner of a room, huddled together. Sometimes we just stand at the side of the road, in a line, watching the traffic, waiting. And always we're laughing, laughing, laughing at what we see. There's no laughing like the laughing of the dead, Michael.

As MOSSY *concludes, the figure of* FR SEAMUS, *dressed in a decent layman's suit, collar and tie, emerges out of the darkness. He watches the two boys for a moment.*

FR SEAMUS   Pay no heed to him, Michael. Let him go back in peace to where he came from.

MICHAEL *starts but never looks directly at* FR SEAMUS.

MICHAEL   Fr Seamus! And you don't stutter anymore!

FR SEAMUS   No. I don't stutter anymore.

MICHAEL   What's going on with me?

FR SEAMUS   You just have to take the next step away from here. And the next step after. And the one after that. But only you can do it, Michael.

MICHAEL   But I don't know who I am or what I am anymore.

FR SEAMUS   You will discover that, Michael. Listen to what the temple of your body is saying to you in secret. Attend to its whispers of hope and desire, streaming through your flesh and blood. It is telling you all you need to know. Go, Michael. Don't look back.

MICHAEL   I'm frightened, so I am —

MOSSY   I'll go, so. If that's what's wanted of me.

MICHAEL   Oh, you are Mossy! Ever the same Mossy. Always giving in. Before you're even started.

MOSSY   I was lying to you, Michael, as per usual!

MICHAEL   What way lying to me?

MOSSY   There's no laughing beyond, no sound at all, just silence —

MICHAEL   (*Cry*) I'll always remember you, Mossy, even if I live to be a hundred! You and Winnie. The two of ye.

MOSSY   (*Departing*) There's nothing beyond the grave, Michael. Nothing at all.

> MOSSY *walks back down the tunnel/cave and it closes up behind him, becoming the ramp once more.*

MICHAEL   (*Yell*) I want to live! I want to live!

FR SEAMUS   Go, Michael! Be true to your own nature. That's all there is, finding one's manhood, finding one's womanhood, and being true to it, no matter what form it takes. That's what salvation is, Michael.

MICHAEL   I know nothing, so I don't —

FR SEAMUS Know nothing! A clean slate! Ignorance is the start of everything, Michael. That's what drives us forward. Questions. Always questions. We are born under the sign of a question-mark, Michael. And that's how we end, too. Questions, questions!

He turns and walks off. For a moment it appears that MICHAEL *might be about to acknowledge the presence of* WINNIE *who is still looking at him. But he walks past her without seeing her and exits. She looks after him and then slowly follows him and the play ends.*